Frequently Asked Questions About ADD
and ADHD
Jonas Pomere
AR B.L.: 8.0 Alt.: 1198
Points: 2.0   UG

FAQ
TEEN LIFE™

FREQUENTLY ASKED QUESTIONS ABOUT

ADD and ADHD

Jonas
Pomere

ROSEN
PUBLISHING®
New York

Published in 2007 by The Rosen Publishing Group, Inc.
29 East 21st Street, New York, NY 10010

Library of Congress Cataloging-in-Publication Data

Pomere, Jonas.
Frequently asked questions about ADD and ADHD / Jonas
Pomere. — 1st ed.
p. cm. — (Faq: teen life)
ISBN-13: 978-1-4042-1970-0
ISBN-10: 1-4042-1970-6
1. Attention deficit hyperactivity disorder—Juvenile literature.
I. Title.
RJ506.H9P66 2007
618.92'8589—dc22

2006033650

Manufactured in the United States of America

Contents

Introduction

Sometimes you may find yourself bombarded by distractions or you may have trouble sitting still in class. And as hectic as life gets, it may sometimes be a feat to keep track of everything, with all the homework, chores, and things you have to do. However, if such difficulties constantly prevent you from tackling what the day brings, you may have attention deficit disorder (ADD) or attention deficit/hyperactivity disorder (ADHD). Having one of these disorders means that your struggles at school and home go much deeper than any combination of forgetfulness, laziness, disorganization, and impatience. In fact, ADD and ADHD are commonly diagnosed in teens, and some believe that these disorders are overdiagnosed. Fortunately, for those who genuinely have ADD and ADHD, there are a variety of effective approaches to treat them.

Symptoms of ADD and ADHD

We all have off days from time to time, when we can't concentrate or we seem to lose track of things. But if you have ADD, you wage a daily battle against a set of specific attention and learning issues. ADD typically begins in childhood, but sometimes the disorder is not diagnosed until the teen years or even later. Some may have ADD and never

Unable to focus or ADD/ADHD? Finding it difficult to pay attention in class can be a symptom of something other than a learning disorder, such as a vision problem.

have it diagnosed, or medically described and identified. A diagnosis of ADD is given only if you have a lifelong history of most of the following symptoms:

- Being easily distracted
- Difficulty paying attention
- Difficulty listening
- Difficulty organizing and completing tasks, projects, and activities
- Avoidance of activities and tasks that require much effort

- Tendency to lose things needed in daily activities
- Tendency to forget things needed in daily activities

ADHD, too, is a disorder that begins in childhood. (ADHD in adults is known as adult attention deficit disorder.) An ADHD diagnosis is given only if a child has a lifelong history of most of the symptoms listed above, plus most of the following symptoms:

- Constant fidgeting, squirming, running, or climbing
- Inability to participate in quiet activities
- Difficulty waiting in turn
- Pushing, shoving, and intruding on others
- Talking excessively

What Causes ADD/ADHD?

ADD and ADHD are both medical, not behavioral, disorders. They are often grouped together and thought of as ADD/ADHD. But there are significant differences between ADD and ADHD.

ADD causes people to be inattentive and easily distracted. With ADHD, people have the qualities of ADD but also are impulsive or hyperactive. Medical scientists think that ADD and ADHD are caused by a chemical imbalance in the brain. The front part of the brain (just behind the forehead) helps you pay attention, concentrate, organize things, and put the brakes on impulsive or unacceptable behavior. In people with ADD or ADHD, the front part of the brain may not be able to use the brain's main signal senders, neurotransmitters, the way it is supposed to. The front

Oppositional defiant disorder (ODD), characterized by frequent temper tantrums, disobedience, and hostility toward authority figures, is present in over half of boys who have ADD/ADHD.

part of the brain has very little to do with intelligence, so it is possible to have ADD or ADHD and still be very smart.

Who Has ADD/ADHD?

Most studies show that between 3 and 5 percent of school-age children are affected by ADD or ADHD. Some studies, however, indicate that as much as 15 percent of the general teen population may be affected. Most children diagnosed with ADD or ADHD are boys. This indicates that boys are more likely than girls to have one of these disorders. However, it is probable that a lot of girls have ADD but go undiagnosed. Why is this the case? It's because the symptoms of ADD and ADHD are different for boys and girls. Some symptoms particular to boys—such as aggressive behavior in ADHD—are more obvious and easier to recognize. For this reason, many more boys than girls are sent for ADD/ADHD testing, and this leads to more boys getting diagnosed. In the United States, there are ten boys recommended for ADD/ADHD testing for each girl recommended.

ADD and ADHD usually show up during the preschool or early grade school years. But for people who are not hyperactive, their ADD can go undiagnosed until they are teens or mature adults. In some cases, people will live their entire lives with ADD or ADHD and never be diagnosed.

Medical research has shown that there is a definite genetic link behind ADD/ADHD. So if one person in a family has one of these disorders, there is a very good chance that someone else in the family had or has it, too.

one

HOW IS ADD/ADHD DIAGNOSED?

It is difficult to diagnose ADD/ADHD because it involves so many different aspects of your personality and behavior. To be more consistent with its diagnoses, the American Academy of Pediatrics recommends using a comprehensive (all-around) assessment that relies on the results of standard tests as well as the input from people who know you well.

Typically, testing to find out if you have ADD/ADHD starts with one or more of the following tests:

1. Intelligence—to evaluate your intelligence quotient (IQ) and reasoning abilities
2. Achievement—to find the actual grade level you're working at
3. Fine motor skills—to see if there are problems with the your hand-eye coordination and/or writing skills

Then, you're evaluated based on the reports and observations of two or more of the following people:

1. Parents—are asked to describe your behavior over a long period of time
2. Teachers—are asked to rate your behavior using standardized forms, and to give their personal opinion of your school work and behavior
3. School counselor—is asked about your overall progress in school and whether there is a history of social or behavior problems
4. You—are asked what you think your problem is, what your thoughts and feelings are, why you think you act the way you do at home and school
5. Family doctor or pediatrician—is asked about your overall health, including vision and hearing, and whether there is a history of medical problems
6. Child psychiatrist (doctor who works with children who have learning and behavioral problems)—may be asked to observe you in both school and nonschool settings and give an opinion on your actions
7. Neurologist (doctor who works with the brain and physical disorders)—may be asked to observe you in school and nonschool settings and give an opinion on physical mobility and coordination

What Diagnosis Means

If you are diagnosed with ADD or ADHD, you now know that your problem is a real medical disorder. That lifts a huge load off

Dealing with ADD/ADHD takes increased parental guidance. One study reports that 52 percent of parents of children with ADHD needed over an hour to help with homework, compared to 28 percent of other parents.

your shoulders by giving you some insight into your academic, social, and family problems. It also means you can start treatments and therapies that can help you manage the disorder.

For your parents, the diagnosis may lift a great load off their shoulders, too. They now know that your learning, concentration, and attention problems are not the result of "bad parenting." The diagnosis also lets them know that there are things they can do to help you do better at home and at school.

For some parents, a diagnosis of ADD or ADHD also starts them thinking about their own childhood and some of the "problems" they had as they were growing up. After their child is diagnosed with ADD or ADHD, many parents say, "That sounds just like me when I was a kid." For some, ADD/ADHD is a disorder they grow out of during adolescence. But about 50 percent of people treated for ADD/ADHD as a child (up to 2.5 percent of the U.S. population) still require medication as adults.

One way that a school can accommodate students with ADD/ADHD is to schedule the subjects they find more difficult in the morning rather than in the afternoon.

For your brothers, sisters, and friends, a diagnosis of ADD or ADHD means there is a real reason—not just a negative attitude, poor motivation, or carelessness—for the way you act. It also means that things probably will be less tense and stressful at home and at school once you begin treatment.

For teachers, a student's diagnosis of ADD or ADHD means that they can make classroom changes and accommodations (different strategies, techniques, and instructional practices) to help you become more successful in school. Diagnosis is a win-win situation for everyone.

two

ARE THERE MEDICATIONS FOR ADD/ADHD?

Attention deficit disorder (ADD) and attention deficit/hyperactivity disorder (ADHD) are medical disabilities, just as nearsightedness is. The medical treatment for nearsightedness is glasses. They don't cure the problem, but they do help bring the world into focus. Treatment for ADD and ADHD can help bring the world into focus, too.

The treatment is multimodal. That means it uses a combination of things to help a person with ADD or ADHD to focus attention and concentration, to minimize impulsive and hyperactive behavior, and to deal with the emotional, social, behavioral, and educational problems that are symptoms of ADD and ADHD.

For most teens with ADD or ADHD, especially those with moderate or severe cases, treatment may begin with medication. Two major classes of medication are used: stimulants and antidepressants.

If medication is effective, multimodal treatment is then expanded. Counseling is a common component of multimodal treatment for a teen with ADD/ADHD, as is behavior modification. For the latter component, negative behaviors are changed by rewarding positive behaviors.

Medication: Part of the Package

Medication will not cure ADD or ADHD, and it will not control emotional or behavioral problems. But it can improve your ability to concentrate and calm down. That makes it easier for you to work on other problems that are part of the ADD/ADHD package. These may include poor social skills, low grades, family problems, or low self-esteem.

ADD/ADHD medication became widespread in the 1980s. Medications seem to work for 75 to 90 percent of the children and teens who try them. Though "meds" are a useful tool in the treatment of ADD/ADHD, there is still a lot of controversy about prescribing them. The major concern of both parents and teens is that the medications used to treat ADD/ADHD are powerful drugs.

Many are concerned about the reported adverse side effects of popular ADD/ADHD medications. For example, prescription stimulants taken for ADD/ADHD are known to cause irregular sleeping patterns, headaches, stomachaches, drowsiness, irritability, and nervousness. More serious side effects have included increased incidence of suicidal thoughts, abnormal

One alternative treatment is the Play Attention helmet, which asks players to control computer images with their minds. Developed by Unique Logic and Technology, founder Peter Freer poses with the interactive learning tool.

thinking, depression, paranoia, and aggression. Other reported health issues in young people include irregular heartbeat and even heart attacks. These reports have alarmed medical professionals and caused them to take more care in prescribing these drugs and to monitor their patients more closely.

Because of the reported negative effects, the federal Food and Drug Administration (FDA) is considering putting a warning on Ritalin and similar stimulant drugs. For their part, drug companies generally maintain that these side effects cannot be definitively blamed on their products. In addition, they point out

Ten Great Questions to Ask Your Doctor If You Have Been Diagnosed with ADD and/or ADHD

1 If I take antidepressants for my ADD/ADHD, will it affect my mood or personality?

2 How soon can I expect medication, counseling, and other kinds of treatment to improve my grades, things at home, and my social life?

3 When taking stimulants like Ritalin, what foods, drinks, drugs, or medications should I avoid?

4 Since ADD/ADHD is a disability, will I be set back a grade or placed in "special" classes?

5 What should I do if my medication's side effects are making me feel worse instead of better?

6 How do I deal with people who pressure me to abuse my ADD/ADHD medication?

7 What other disorders are similar to ADD/ADHD?

8 Why can't my friends use my ADD/ADHD medication every once in a while, to help them stay up all night to study for a big exam or finish an important project?

9 Will I build a tolerance to ADD/ADHD medication?

10 Is there a way to prevent ADD/ADHD?

that the vast majority of young people who use their products have had positive results.

Another concern regarding ADD/ADHD drugs is that a doctor may prescribe too much medication or he or she may prescribe medication when it is not necessary. Some parents also fear that use of drugs for a medical disorder may lead to drug addiction. This fear is not unfounded, as commonly prescribed ADD/ADHD drugs are stimulants, drugs that affect the nervous system and enhance alertness. When abused by people who don't have ADD/ADHD, such drugs produce feel-good effects similar to such illegal stimulants as methamphetamine and cocaine.

These are very real concerns. However, the drugs used to treat ADD and ADHD are not, in themselves, addictive. When they are prescribed by a knowledgeable doctor and taken under the supervision of a responsible adult (such as a parent or school nurse), there is little chance that too much medication may be given or taken. Responsible doctors will make sure that the drug is safe and appropriate for their patients by screening for potential health problems prior to prescribing them. They will then closely monitor the dosage and the effects of the medications.

Finding the Right Medication

"When a medication works, it works almost immediately. There are positive changes right off the bat," says Dr. Julie Wilson, a child psychologist at Brown University School of Medicine.

Of the stimulants, Ritalin, Dexedrine, and Cylert seem to be the medications that work the best for people with ADD or ADHD. Between 70 and 75 percent of people diagnosed with ADD or ADHD have success with one of these three medications. All three of these drugs are stimulants, but they are different chemically. Ritalin is the brand name of a drug known as methylphenidate; Dexedrine is a brand name of the drug dextroamphetamine sulfate; and Cylert is a brand name of the drug pemoline. Other medications with different formulas may be prescribed as well.

In people who do not have ADD or ADHD, stimulants cause many of the symptoms of ADD and ADHD—hyperactivity, nervousness, and inability to concentrate. Doctors do not fully understand why stimulants work differently for people with ADD and ADHD. However, they think stimulants help the brain "put on the brakes."

Dopamine and Stimulants

Why do stimulants work for people with ADD/ADHD? Doctors think people with these disorders have a dopamine imbalance. Dopamine is a chemical in the brain that affects movement, the sense of pleasure, and motivation. Drugs like Ritalin, Dexedrine, and Cylert increase the production of dopamine. When that happens, a person is better able to calm down and focus attention.

The most common stimulants used to treat ADD/ADHD are Ritalin and Dexedrine. They are pills that begin working thirty to forty-five minutes after you take them. Their effects last for only three to four hours. That is why you need to take a "booster" pill at lunchtime. It is also why you may need another pill if you are going to do an evening activity—a homework project, play in a basketball game—that requires focus and concentration.

In March 2006, the FDA approved the first prescription patch to treat ADD/ADHD. It contains a formula similar to Ritalin and is applied to the skin, like a Band-Aid. The ADD/ADHD patch is meant to be worn for nine hours, which is better than taking pills for patients who may forget or have to go to the nurse's office to take pills.

The other common stimulant is Cylert. It acts more slowly than Dexedrine or Ritalin, but the effect usually lasts nine to twelve hours. That can be a definite plus in school, or on long car trips. Another popular ADHD medication, Adderall, is a stimulant that is chemically different from Dexedrine, Cylert, and

Ritalin. Its formula combines several different chemicals in an extended-release tablet that can be effective for more than twelve hours.

Antidepressants and ADD/ADHD Treatment

Stimulants do not work for everyone with ADD or ADHD. They may have little or no effect on concentration or hyperactive behavior. Or they may produce unpleasant side effects such as headaches or weight loss. In cases like these, some doctors prescribe antidepressants instead of stimulants to treat ADD/ADHD. These include Tofranil, Norpramin, and Prozac.

When used to treat ADD/ADHD, antidepressants produce most of the same effects as stimulants. Some antidepressants also seem to help other problems that sometimes accompany ADD or ADHD. For example, antidepressants may help control bedwetting and sleepwalking, two disorders associated with dopamine imbalances.

Medication Pluses and Minuses

The stimulants and antidepressants commonly used for ADD or ADHD have both pluses and minuses.

The pluses include:
- Increased ability to concentrate and focus attention
- Less overall restlessness and hyperactivity
- Less impulsive behavior

- Less aggressive behavior
- Improved grades in school
- Improved social interaction

The minuses include:
- Appetite and weight loss
- Inability to sleep through the night
- Headaches or stomachaches
- Sleepiness
- Sadness or irritability, especially when the medication wears off
- Increased hyperactivity, especially when the medication wears off

Dangerous side effects that should be carefully considered along with the child's or teen's health history include:
- Abnormal heartbeat
- High blood pressure
- Increased risk of heart attacks
- Paranoia
- Aggressive behavior
- Depression

ADD/ADHD medications can alter a person's sleeping patterns and contribute to increased sleepiness during the day, affecting classroom performance.

The Center for Attention Related Disorders runs a four-week camp in New Fairfield, Connecticut, for youths with ADD/ADHD. The camp's regimented environment can be attributed to the fact that the camp provides one counselor for every two campers.

Is Medication Forever?

For many people with ADD or ADHD, medication is not a forever-after matter. Many doctors suggest "medication vacations," so teens often do not take medication after school, on weekends, during school vacations, or in the summertime. Also, some people with mild cases of ADD or ADHD outgrow many of their symptoms—restlessness, talkativeness, lack of organization, poor grades, poor social skills—in their late teens. When that happens, they often discontinue taking medication.

Omega 3 plays an important role in brain function and is found to be deficient in people with ADD/ADHD. Snacking on walnuts is a tasty way to get this essential fatty acid.

In general, however, about half the people who take medication for ADD or ADHD continue taking it, either regularly or when they are involved in special projects, into adulthood.

Your Diet and ADD/ADHD

Although it's a well-known fact that fatty foods should be eaten sparingly, the lack of monounsaturated ("good") fats in a person's diet can affect health. In fact, some studies have shown that children and teens with ADD/ADHD are commonly deficient in the good fat omega 3, an essential fatty acid. Therefore, some researchers recommend that children and teens with ADD/ADHD add foods rich in omega 3 to their diets. Omega 3 can be found in fish oil, cod liver oil, and flax seed. Cooking with olive oil and eating nuts with good fats (walnuts, almonds, and macadamias) is also recommended.

three

HOW CAN COUNSELING, THERAPY, AND BEHAVIOR MODIFICATION HELP?

For most teens with attention deficit disorder (ADD) or attention deficit/hyperactivity disorder (ADHD), counseling is a very important part of managing their condition. Counseling is talking to a qualified professional, such as a therapist or counselor, on a regular (usually weekly) basis. Also called "therapy," counseling lets you talk out your problems, fears, hopes, dreads, and dreams in a nonjudgmental setting. It helps you uncover any feelings of confusion, impatience, frustration, anger, resentment, fear, hurt, shame, or guilt because of your medical condition. It also helps you discover strengths you didn't know you had. Many with ADD/ADHD are uncommonly sensitive to others and are highly creative, energetic, enthusiastic, and adaptable.

If you have especially personal issues or emotions to express about having ADD/ADHD, one-on-one counseling may be more beneficial to you than a peer group setting.

In counseling, you and the counselor sometimes playact family or school problems or social situations. When you "act out" things that have been bugging and bothering you, you often find that they aren't as bad as you thought. At other times you discover that problems really are as bad as they seem, but two heads— yours and the counselor's—can solve them more easily and faster.

Sometimes counseling is done in peer group sessions. In this kind of counseling, teens who have similar challenges and have faced many of the same situations are able to share solutions and insights.

At other times, counseling may include other family members. It is important for them to participate in counseling, too. Even though they do not have the disorder, they are still affected by it.

What Is Behavior Modification?

In order to get the full benefits of a multimodal treatment plan, people with ADD or ADHD need to combine counseling with

Your cell phone not only keeps you connected to friends, it can connect you to tutoring, advice, and encouragement when you're also tackling complicated math equations.

behavior changes. These changes allow positive behaviors to replace the negative behaviors and attitudes that have built up over the years.

Attitude and behavior changes, especially major ones, won't just happen on their own. They must be shoehorned into your daily life through the use of what psychologists call behavior modification therapy.

Counseling helps you get in touch with your thoughts and feelings. Behavior modification, on the other hand, helps you develop new (and better) behaviors to replace your old feelings, attitudes, and behaviors, which may be self-destructive.

For example, if you constantly get flustered when working on complicated math problems, you could learn to count to ten and take a break so that frustration doesn't lead to giving up. You could also make it a habit to slow down and do math problems one step at a time. And perhaps you could effectively help change unproductive behavior by giving yourself a small reward when you succeed at a task. For example, you could go to the movies with friends or go to the local skate park after successfully finishing your math homework for a week.

Think of behavior modification as self-training for people with ADD/ADHD. It helps you do the right thing in everyday situations as well as in situations that are new to you.

When you are learning behavior modification techniques, you usually have to stop and think about every little move you make. After a while, however, the new ways of thinking and feeling and acting become so natural that they kick in on their own.

Occupational Therapy and ADD/ADHD

Occupational therapy (OT) is another type of therapy that significantly reduces the negative behaviors associated with ADD/ADHD. In particular, OT helps you control stimulation related to sight, sound, smell, and touch (called sensory stimulation).

Under normal conditions, people process and adapt to sensory stimulation in their environment. This process is called sensory integration. But if you have ADD/ADHD, you are unable to adapt properly to the stimulation. Instead, you become easily overstimulated. You might become so distracted by a sound or movement that you cannot keep your train of thought on the rails. In the classroom, for example, you might focus so intently on an ambulance siren outside that it's impossible for you to pay attention to the teacher. In such cases, occupational therapy can be tailored to your needs to help you develop skills and strategies to deal with sensory information.

Typical OC techniques involve making the person more aware of body posture, balance, and physical positioning. In addition, for some teens, lightly brushing the skin, deeply rubbing certain muscles, or squeezing an exercise ball can help them maintain concentration. Those who need oral stimulation are encouraged to chew gum or bite on a rubber tube when they need to concentrate. Several recent studies have clearly shown that children and teens who work with occupational therapists are more at ease in stimulating environments and can pay better attention in a noisy classroom.

Find a Coach

It is possible to change some negative ADD/ADHD behaviors on your own. It's easier and faster, however, if you work with someone who can help you stick with the program. That means finding a personal "coach."

A coach isn't a substitute parent or a personal nag. He or she is someone who will:

- Help you practice positive, new ways to deal with negative, old behaviors
- Offer suggestions, advice, reminders, support, and (most important of all) encouragement
- Help you get organized so you can set and reach goals
- Help you recognize successes (and near successes)
- Help you deal with failures (and figure out why they occurred)

Having a mentor can provide the boost you need to overcome the obstacles of ADD/ADHD. You can find mentor programs at your school, community library, or local YMCA.

A coach should be someone that you like, but he or she should also be a "neutral" person. The best coaches are people who are firm and fair. They will be strict and tough on you if that is what is needed to keep you headed in the right direction.

Though parents, siblings, and friends should work with the coach, in most cases they do not make good coaches. Who then?

It definitely should be someone you respect and who cares about and respects you. That could be a teacher, a school guidance counselor, a therapist, or a close family friend. It could be an adult you know through your church or synagogue, or through community organizations such as the recreation center or "Y," Boys and Girls Clubs, Boy Scouts or Girl Scouts, Big Brothers/Big Sisters, or 4-H. Making an appointment to discuss this with any of these trusted adults, especially your school counselor or therapist, may be the best way to begin this search. Also, ADD/ADHD support groups with Web sites have great resources and may have useful recommendations for you.

four

ARE THERE STRATEGIES THAT CAN HELP AT HOME AND SCHOOL?

The major symptoms of attention deficit disorder (ADD) and attention deficit/hyperactivity disorder (ADHD) are forgetfulness, lack of organization, impulsiveness, and poor people skills. Learning coping strategies and techniques for dealing with these symptoms can completely turn things around at home. They make your home a lot less stressful because they add structure, order, and success to your life.

Improving Things on the Home Front

Learning home-front coping skills isn't something that can be done alone. To find successful ways to deal with the baggage that comes along with ADD or ADHD, you need to do some reading. You also need to work cooperatively with your parents and siblings, and you may need to work with a counselor or coach, too.

In the meantime, here are some techniques and strategies that will immediately help you turn things around at home.

> **Get organized.** It is easier to keep track of things and keep organized if similar things are stored together. In the closet, shirts should go with shirts, pants with pants, and so on.
>
> **Make lists.** Once a day, or once a week, make a list of the activities and chores—ranked from most important to least important—that you need to do. Always check things off so you will see what you have accomplished.
>
> **Create routines.** Do things that you have to do on a daily or weekly basis—take out the trash, deliver neighborhood newspapers, mow the lawn—at the same time, in the same way, every time you do them.
>
> **Keep a "my stuff" box** at the foot of the stairs or near the front door. Put things you need to carry upstairs or take with you when you leave the house.
>
> **Learn to negotiate.** If there are problems with family members, hold family meetings to solve them. During these sessions, negotiate trade-offs (win-win situations) that solve the problems. For instance, get your parents to agree to let you have a swim party on the weekend (you win!) if you keep your room clean all week (they win!).

One way you can keep your list close to you wherever you go is to place it with important everyday items, such as your keys or wallet.

Exercise. Running, in-line skating, or doing other aerobic exercises will help you keep in shape and reduce stress. Exercise also releases a natural feel-good hormone, serotonin, into the body.

Making School Work for You, Not Against You

In most schools, every student is required to sit still at a desk, pay attention to the lessons and to the teacher, and cooperate

Myths and Facts About ADD/ADHD

 ADD/ADHD gives kids an excuse for their unmotivated behavior. Fact ➡ An ADD/ADHD diagnosis provides possible solutions, not excuses, for what is not just "unmotivated" behavior. Treatment usually involves counseling, coaching, and/or behavioral modification to overcome bad habits, lack of organization, and negative thoughts.

 Ritalin and other stimulant drugs used to treat ADD/ADHD are just like methamphetamines and cocaine. Fact ➡ Ritalin and other stimulants prescribed by doctors help kids with ADD/ADHD calm down, focus, and be more productive. Those who get high from and abuse these drugs do not have ADD/ADHD.

 Eating too much sugar causes ADHD. Fact ➡ There is no scientific evidence of a connection between sugar and ADHD.

Herbal and vitamin supplements can successfully treat ADD/ADHD. Fact ➤ There is no scientific proof that herbal and vitamin "miracle" supplements work for ADD/ADHD.

People with ADD/ADHD never grow up to be successful. Fact ➤ People with ADD or ADHD have traits related to their disorder that can be assets. Famous, successful people with ADHD include actor Jim Carrey and software giant Bill Gates. Emily Dickinson, one of the greatest poets of the twentieth century, exhibited traits of ADD/ADHD, too.

with teachers, students, and "the system." These are the very things that a student with ADD or ADHD can't do.

This means that students with ADD and ADHD have major challenges at school. It also means that a teacher is often the first one to suggest a test for ADD or ADHD.

Teachers can be your best allies if you have ADD or ADHD. Students with these disorders need their teachers' understanding, cooperation, and classroom accommodations in order to do their best.

Tackling School Problems

If you have ADD or ADHD, it's a good idea to make an appointment with all your teachers at the beginning of each school year.

Sitting at the head of the class if you have ADD/ADHD can help a lot. Not only will it reduce distractions, it can also increase your class participation.

Talk with them about your condition. With some teachers, you can make a "learning contract." This is an agreement listing the steps you are both going to take to help you succeed in class.

Here are some proven self-management, organizational, and study strategies that work for students and teachers. Use as many of them as you can.

Sit in the front of the class so you are not distracted by other students and so the teacher can see when you do not understand something.

Organize notebooks and folders. Have separate, different-colored folders for each class. Divide folders into three sections. Use the front section to record homework assignments, and check off when they are done. Use the middle section for notes and class work. Use the last section to store returned homework and tests that you should review for final exams.

Take notes your way. When a class requires a lot of notes, write down important and/or key words, then borrow and photocopy a classmate's or the teacher's notes. In foreign language class, or in classes where there is a lot of information, use a tape recorder. Then listen to the tape at home and take notes at your own speed.

Ask for extra time to do your assignments and, especially, take tests. If possible, take tests orally. But make sure that when you set extended deadlines, you are able to meet them.

Get feedback. Ask the teacher for a checklist of your most common written mistakes. Use it to proofread homework, and if possible, the work done in class.

Tips for Homework Success

Academic success isn't built only on what you do in the classroom. It's built on homework, too. There is a lot you can do at home to make sure that homework and special projects are done well and turned in on time.

Create a school calendar. Purchase a large wall calendar and write down all your school-related activities—homework assignments, tests, special projects, contests, and programs. Use it to help you schedule study time for tests and pace yourself so you do not have several things due on the same day.

Have a special place for homework. Keep it stocked with school "tools"—pens, correction fluid, a dictionary, a calculator. If possible, keep copies of school textbooks here, too.

Manage your time. Do only one thing at a time, and pace work by breaking assignments down into smaller parts. For example, if you have a report due in two weeks, spend a couple of nights doing research, then schedule another couple of nights to organize information and outline the report. Give yourself a week to actually write the report. And finally, spend one evening, a couple of nights before it is due, proofreading it.

Use a kitchen timer or alarm clock to help you set and meet timed deadlines for completing homework assignments, or parts of them. When you have finished a timed assignment, take a break to give your brain a breather.

Use aids to help you remember things. Make and use flash cards for foreign language class. If you learn better when you hear things, read text assignments and notes into a tape recorder and play them back. When memorizing, turn information into silly sentences or words. For instance, HOMES isn't lots of houses, it's the Great Lakes (Huron, Ontario, Michigan, Erie, Superior).

Improve your proofreading skills. Always go over homework a second time. If possible, do all written work on a computer, then use punctuation, grammar, and spell-check

Where you study can be as important as how you study. If distractions at home, such as TV and the Internet, are a problem for you, try studying at the library.

functions to check your work. If you do not have a computer, read homework out loud or from the bottom up. Both systems help you catch errors.

Your Legal Rights at School

ADD and ADHD interfere with the ability to learn and interact with others, so the United States Department of Education (DOE) considers them disabilities "which adversely affect . . . educational performance."

People with ADD and ADHD qualify for special, free services from their schools. This right is guaranteed by two U.S. laws: the Individuals with Disabilities Education Act (Part B) and the Vocational Rehabilitation Act (Section 504). In most cases, these services include:

- Medical diagnosis, by the school system, of ADD or ADHD
- Creation of an individual educational program (IEP)—with

input from school counselors, teachers, school administrators, and parents—to meet an ADD or ADHD student's unique educational needs

➤ Reasonable accommodations—such as seating changes, additional time for tests, or the substitution of oral for written work—to aid in educational performance

➤ These services are usually available until a person reaches the age of twenty-one or leaves school, so they are available in college and technical school, too.

Some schools are underfunded and overcrowded. In addition, sometimes the teaching staff has difficulties finding the resources to help their students with ADD/ADHD. If you are in such a school system, you may have problems getting the special services to which you are entitled. Don't hesitate to ask your parents to be assertive spokespersons, or advocates, for you. They can write detailed letters, make phone calls, and/or visit your school on a regular basis to keep your program on track.

Dealing with the Pressure to Share Your Meds

People without ADD/ADHD can get high from abusing drugs prescribed specifically for you. If you are using Ritalin or Adderall, you might find yourself under pressure by some cliques or new "friends" to share or sell your medication. Not only will this drain the supply of medication you need, sharing and selling it can get you into serious trouble and put other people's health at risk.

If you have just been prescribed ADD/ADHD medication, it's best not to announce your use and to avoid people you think might take advantage of you. The instant "popularity" you might gain from sharing or selling your medication may seem tempting. But the truth is that people suddenly asking you to hang out or to go to parties because you have pills to party with are more interested in getting high than being your friend. Other people might say they need your meds to study and get through a big test, but if they really needed it, they'd have their own prescriptions.

If people already know you're taking ADD/ADHD meds and you're beginning to feel the pressure to share them, you should let them know that your use is strictly monitored. For instance, tell them that each time you take a pill at school, the nurse must watch you swallow it and that your parents keep count of the pills you have left and only give you what you need each day. If people begin to harass you for your meds, don't hesitate to talk to a teacher or counselor about what's going on.

five

CAN I TAKE CONTROL OF MY LIFE BACK?

Many people whose attention deficit disorder (ADD) or attention deficit/hyperactivity disorder (ADHD) is not recognized until they are in their late teens may have already lost much self-esteem. Their undiagnosed disorder may have already caused them frustration, anxiety, anger, and embarrassment. It may have got them teased, picked on, nagged, and grounded. It may have contributed to many of their failures— flunked tests, failed friendships, or a flubbed driver's license test. It may also have caused them many personal problems with family, friends, and teachers. It may even have led to trouble with the law.

It is possible to rebuild self-confidence, self-esteem, and feelings of self-worth after a diagnosis of ADD or ADHD. And it is easier than you think. But rebuilding takes time, effort, and confidence that change is possible.

Rebuilding self-esteem and self-confidence does not mean getting back at people or becoming a superteen. It does mean seeing the positives that ADD or ADHD carry with them, and discovering the real you.

Recognize Strengths

If you have ADD or ADHD, you know all about the problems it can cause. However, many of these "problems" have flip sides that carry some wonderful hidden strengths. For instance, the inability to focus on one thing at a time becomes a strength if you turn it into the ability to adjust to constantly changing situations. A constant need to be on the go is a strength when you funnel it into sports, scientific research, or other high-focus/high-energy activities. Daydreaming is a strength when you employ it in artistic or creative situations.

The following traits are often part of the ADD or ADHD package. But by re-framing the way you think about them, you can begin to view these "negatives" as their positive flip sides:

- Some may say you are a slow worker, but you know that you are *detail-oriented, careful, and very observant.*
- You are not withdrawn; *you are a deep or careful thinker and critical-minded.*
- You are not judgmental; instead you are *committed to fairness and justice.*
- You are not easily hurt, but you are *attuned to others' feelings and needs.*

Your constant need to be on the move can be a great advantage in athletics. Maximize this dynamic asset by joining the football team or getting involved in other fast-paced sports.

> Don't think of yourself as impatient; instead you are a *solution seeker and a problem solver.*

> If someone says you are a nonvisual learner, let them know you are *able to learn through other senses.*

Tips for Building Self-Esteem and Self-Confidence

Educating yourself about your ADD or ADHD can help rebuild feelings of self-confidence and personal satisfaction. Like they say, "Knowledge is power." The more you know about your medical condition and how to manage its symptoms, the more confident you can become. Think of the following tips as a way to discover the real person who may be buried under the extra baggage that comes along with ADD/ADHD:

Psych yourself up for a new you. Use mental imaging to paint a picture of a new you—having better relationships with family members, making better grades, working at a part-time job.

Set reasonable goals. It's good to have goals and dreams. But be sure to set realistic ones.

Give yourself constructive criticism. When you don't achieve a goal, don't beat yourself up. Look closely at why you failed—poor organization, aiming too high, not enough hard work—and use failure as a teaching experience.

Join a peer support group. Sharing your experiences with peers who are dealing with similar problems can give you new strategies and resources.

Join "fun" groups. Clubs and groups are peer support groups, but they are fun. At school, the debate or drama club may be intimidating if you are shy, but the journalism club, chess club, or drill team won't be. If you like to help others, look into volunteering.

Take up a sport or hobby. Sports and hobbies can help you work off pent-up physical or mental energy, and redirect it in constructive ways.

As self-esteem, self-confidence, and feelings of self-worth grow, they feed off each other. Strength leads to strength. As you

10 FACTS ABOUT
ADD and ADHD

1 ADD/ADHD affects the front part of the brain; this part controls the ability to focus, organize, and pay attention.

2 Conservative estimates say that 3 to 5 percent of school-age children are affected by ADD or ADHD.

3 Boys tend to be hyperactive more than girls.

4 Stimulants and antidepressants are the major types of medication used to treat ADD/ADHD.

5 Medications for ADD/ADHD seem to work for 75 to 90 percent of people who try them.

6 People diagnosed with ADD or ADHD are successfully treated with stimulants such as Ritalin, Dexedrine, and Cylert in 70 to 75 percent of the cases.

7 About half the people who take medication for ADD or ADHD continue taking it when they are adults.

8 ADD/ADHD seems to be the result of problems with a person's neurotransmitters—the brain's primary signal senders.

9 Medical research suggests genetics play a factor in who has ADD/ADHD.

10 According to one recent study, 95 percent of the subjects with ADHD who underwent occupational therapy showed clear improvements in their abilities to block out distractions in the classroom.

become surer of yourself, you become less angry, anxious, and reactive about your ADD or ADHD, and more proactive about yourself.

ADD/ADHD and the Social Scene

We all like to feel accepted by friends and peers; we all like to belong to a group. Whether you realize it or not, friends and peers are very important to your identity and self-esteem. They listen to you and accept and understand your challenges and concerns. If you are like most teens, your friendships are probably as important to you as your family relationships.

Making Friends

Making and keeping friends can be a special challenge if you have ADD or ADHD. A study by the American Academy of Child and Adolescent Psychiatry indicated that adolescents with

ADD and ADHD tend to have fewer friends than peers without these conditions. Several factors may explain this finding.

First, some teens with ADD or ADHD feel that it makes them "different," and this feeling leads them to avoid people and social situations altogether. Others may find that their friends disapprove of them when their ADD or ADHD causes them to behave in distracting or age-inappropriate ways. This situation, too, may cause teens with ADD/ADHD to become less active socially.

It's not easy to accept feeling like an outsider or losing friends because of your ADD or ADHD. But it is important to understand that all teens in all different social groups go through feelings of rejection and uncertainty. In the end, it's important for you to create and maintain friendships with people who value you as an individual.

Take note if you find yourself changing the way you dress, talk, or act based on the people you hang around with. Feeling like an "outsider" is no fun, but the situation will only get worse if you try to make new friendships based mostly on your desire to fit in. Instead, take the opportunity to examine your own values, and then seek out friends who seem to have the same values. If you do find someone who you would like to hang out with, try to be interested in who they are and what they like. There's no need to rush into a friendship, so give your new friend some room and let the relationship grow naturally.

ADD/ADHD and Dating

Just as making and keeping everyday friends can be difficult, it can be equally challenging to find and keep a regular boyfriend

You may feel that having ADD/ADHD sets you apart from other people, so it's important to build friendships where differences are accepted and there's no pressure to fit in.

or girlfriend. If you are a teen with ADD or ADHD, you probably already know this from experience. Your experience is backed up by studies that show teens with ADD and ADHD tend to have more dating partners than peers without these conditions. And the dating relationships they *do* have tend not to last as long.

If you are interested in someone, it's up to you whether you want to tell them you have ADD or ADHD. If you do tell a potential boyfriend or girlfriend about your ADD/ADHD, it sometimes helps to compare it to a more common condition that requires correction, such as being nearsighted or farsighted. Like glasses, medication helps your condition.

> Before getting serious, make sure your dating partner respects the fact that you have a learning disorder and doesn't try to take advantage of or use it against you.

It is important that a new friend, or a new boyfriend or girlfriend, accept you as you are. If you start changing just so that someone will accept you, you will have a hard time sorting out your real friends. When it comes to dating, girls with ADD or ADHD should be especially careful not to use sex as a tool for gaining acceptance from boys. Studies show that teen girls with ADD or ADHD tend to have more sexual partners than peers who don't have these conditions. As a result, females with ADD/ADHD become mothers at a younger age and are also more likely to contract a sexually transmitted disease than girls in the non-ADD/ADHD group. Let your values, rather than your condition, control the decisions you make.

Just Like People Without ADD or ADHD

If you have been diagnosed with attention deficit disorder (ADD) or attention deficit/hyperactivity disorder (ADHD), you have been given a name and, more important, a treatment plan for the problem that has been running your life. But it also creates questions related to who you are and who you want to become.

- People with ADD and ADHD have a wide variety of intellectual abilities, special talents, and unique interests—just like people without ADD or ADHD.
- People with ADD or ADHD have personalities that range from life of the party to wallflower—just like people without ADD or ADHD.
- People with ADD or ADHD range from being workaholics to slackers—just like people without ADD or ADHD.

And although ADD and ADHD are medical disabilities, when they are managed, they are definitely not a handicap in the career world. That means that when you are planning a career, you bring to a job search the same abilities, characteristics, and capabilities as someone who doesn't have ADD or ADHD.

ADD/ADHD and Driving

In the majority of situations, people with ADD or ADHD are no different from those without these disorders. However, research indicates that this is not the case when it comes to driving a motor vehicle. The American Academy of Pediatrics studied a group of people with ADHD between the ages of sixteen and twenty-two. The study found that those with ADHD were more

Like being nearsighted, having ADD/ADHD is a medical problem that can hinder your driving. Therefore, it's especially important that you stay focused when you're behind the wheel.

likely than those without the disorder to have crashes. They were also more likely to be at fault in crashes. In addition, young drivers with ADHD were more likely to receive traffic citations, especially for speeding and reckless driving. Other studies have shown that driving difficulties continue into adulthood for people with ADHD.

In order to drive safely, you need to be able to focus on your own vehicle, while also paying attention to driving conditions. Drivers regularly have to deal with poor road conditions, heavy traffic, signal lights and honking horns, and numerous roadside distractions. Unfortunately, for drivers with ADD or ADHD, these conditions are precisely the ones that are especially challenging. A momentary distraction is all it takes for a driver to end up causing an accident. The following tips may help you become a safer, better driver:

➤ Driving is a privilege, not a right. Take your responsibility seriously.

➤ Know where you are going, and plan trips in advance. Use familiar roads whenever possible. Being late for school or an appointment can be a distraction in itself.

➤ Limit the distractions in the car while driving. For example, leave your cell phone, pager, text-messaging devices, etc., in the trunk. It will be there for you in an emergency, but you will not be distracted by its ringing.

➤ Limit the decisions you have to make while driving, especially the ones not directly related to the task of driving. For instance, decide to listen to CDs rather than the radio. This will keep you from wanting to change the station. Make a mix tape that has only the songs you like. Set the temperature at a comfortable level and then forget about it.

➤ Whenever possible, plan to drive when traffic is light.

➤ Don't overestimate your driving abilities. If everyone else complains about your driving habits, chances are you are not a good driver! Be smart; let a friend drive, or carpool whenever possible.

After High School

Most well-paying jobs require post–high school training at a technical school, junior college, or four-year college. So you should definitely consider more education after high school.

That's not as difficult as you may think. Many schools have programs and curriculums that can meet the special needs of people with ADD or ADHD. In fact, technical schools and the technical programs at two-year colleges, with their shorter programs and hands-on learning, have always offered very good learning environments to people with ADD or ADHD. Some four-year colleges also have programs that are set up to meet the needs of people with ADD or ADHD.

When you begin looking at post–high school career options, keep two things in mind:

- The career you choose should give you a chance to minimize your weaknesses and maximize your strengths, especially your unique ability to look at situations creatively and tap into your very high energy levels.
- With or without post–high school training, people with ADD or ADHD usually have only limited success in careers that require lots of hands-on paperwork. For that reason, careers that require a lot of recordkeeping, or highly detailed documentation—such as travel agent, executive secretary, or tax accountant—probably are not good choices.

Good Career Choices

When people with ADD have learned to use special organization and time management techniques, they are often successful as hotel, resort, or restaurant managers; police officers or private detectives; freelance writers or newspaper reporters; computer operators or programmers; building contractors or construction project managers; scientific researchers; corporate lawyers; and business and educational consultants.

People with ADD/ADHD may be suited for careers on the front line, where change happens quickly and risks must be taken, such as emergency medical services or law enforcement.

People with ADD are often empathetic, meaning that they tend to see and understand the feelings and needs of others. Because of this, they also do very well in the caring professions, where they make excellent customer-service representatives, airline attendants, social workers, hospice nurses, and teachers.

In addition, people with ADHD tend to be outgoing, high-energy, action-seeking people. Since they like excitement and new things, many choose careers that give them lots of freedom to move around at work or to travel, experience new situations, and interact with a variety of people. That is why many become very successful actors or musicians, professional athletes, trial lawyers, and politicians.

People with ADHD also are successful in careers that require a lot of instantaneous decision making, crisis management, or troubleshooting, such as emergency room doctor or nurse, emergency medical services (EMS) technician, emergency repair technician, commercial airline pilot, or radio announcer or disk jockey.

Not surprisingly, since they are always seeing things in new ways, people with ADHD are successful as fiction writers, fashion and industrial designers, marketing and public relations specialists, salespeople, and motivational speakers. And because they are able to process many things at once, many people with ADHD become artists or inventors.

Looking Ahead

With hard work and support, you will be able not only to "just get by" through school but to follow your dreams wherever they lead you. You may find that what you thought were your ADD or ADHD "negatives" will, in the long run, help you become the best person you can be.

attention deficit disorder (ADD) A mild to severe medical disorder that is characterized by the inability to focus, concentrate, and pay attention for long periods of time.

attention deficit/hyperactivity disorder (ADHD) Attention deficit disorder (see above) accompanied by impulsivity and overactivity.

behavior modification Skills, strategies, and techniques that help change and modify the negative behaviors and attitudes that often accompany ADD or ADHD.

counselor A professional who works with people to help them understand their feelings and solve their problems.

diagnosis Identification and description of a medical condition or problem.

empathetic To be tuned in to and responsive to the feelings of others.

hyperactivity Excessively active, restless, and impulsive behavior.

impulsive Acting or speaking without thinking or considering consequences.

inattentive Easily distracted; unable to pay attention.

low self-esteem Lack of confidence or faith in one's capabilities.

multimodal treatment Treatment of a medical disorder that uses more than one method, program, or approach at the same time.

neurotransmitter Chemical substance produced by the body that acts as a messenger or signal carrier.

peer group People, usually of the same age and grade, who have many things in common.

peer group support A group of people with many of the same problems or goals who share information, insights, and feelings in a group setting.

prioritize To organize and rank tasks, problems, or projects according to their importance.

self-confidence Trust or faith in oneself and one's abilities.

self-esteem Feelings of confidence and personal worth.

sibling A brother or sister.

stimulant A medication or drug that increases energy and mental activity.

symptom Characteristic or condition that results from or accompanies a disease or disorder. Symptoms help to diagnose many diseases and illnesses.

therapist Person—counselor, social worker, psychologist, or psychiatrist—who is specially trained to treat a disease or physical or mental condition.

therapy Treatment of an injury, disease, or mental disorder.

These agencies and organizations can supply you with more
information on attention deficit disorder (ADD) and attention
deficit/hyperactivity disorder (ADHD) and put you in touch
with ADD/ADHD support groups in your area.

ADD Warehouse (catalog and supplies)
300 Northwest 70th Avenue, Suite 102
Plantation, FL 33317
(800) 233-9273
Web site: http://www.addwarehouse.com
  ADD Warehouse provides a variety of different educational
  and training books, videos, and other materials on ADD/
  ADHD for teens and parents.

Children and Adults with Attention Deficit Disorder (CHAAD)
8181 Professional Place, Suite 150
Landover, MD 20785
(800) 233-4050
Web site: http://www.chadd.org
  With 20,000 members, CHADD is a one of the largest
  nonprofit organizations dedicated to serving the needs of
  children, teens, and adults with ADD/ADHD.

Learning Disabilities Association of America (LDA)
4156 Library Road
Pittsburgh, PA 15234-1349

(412) 341-1515

Web site: http://www.ldaamerica.org

Founded in 1963, LDA is a major nonprofit volunteer organization advocating for individuals with learning disabilities. LDA has more than 40,000 members in twenty-seven countries around the world.

National Center for Learning Disabilities (NCLD)

381 Park Avenue South, Suite 1401

New York, NY 10016

(888) 575-7373

Web site: http://www.ncld.org

The NCLD is an organization working to ensure that the nation's 15 million children, teens, and adults with learning disabilities have every opportunity to succeed in school, work, and life.

Web Sites

Due to the changing nature of Internet links, Rosen Publishing has developed an online list of Web sites related to the subject of this book. This site is updated regularly. Please use this link to access the list:

http://www.rosenlinks.com/faq/adhd

For Further Reading

Fox, Janet S. *Get Organized Without Losing It.*
Minneapolis, MN: Free Spirit Publishing, 2006.

Halliwell, Edward M., MD, and John J. Ratey, MD. *Driven to Distraction: Recognizing and Coping with Attention Deficit Disorder from Childhood Through Adulthood.*
New York, NY: Touchstone, 1995.

Paquette, Penny Hutchins. *Learning Disabilities: The Ultimate Teen Guide* (It Happened to Me). Lanham, MD: Scarecrow Press, Inc., 2003.

Strong, Jeff, Michael O. Flanagan, and Lito Tajeda-Flores. *ADD/ADHD for Dummies.* Hoboken, NJ: John Wiley & Sons, 2004.

Zeigler Dendy, Chris A., and Alex Zeigler. *A Bird's-Eye View of Life with ADD and ADHD: Advice from Young Survivors.* Cedar Bluff, AL: Cherish the Children, 2003.

Bibliography

"ADD, ADHD and Omega-3s—Something's Fishy." *Metro Pulse,* Vol. 15, No. 5, February 5, 2005. Retrieved October 2006 (http://www.metropulse.com/dir_zine/dir_2005/dir_1505/t_newhealth.html).

Barkley, Russel A. *Taking Charge of ADHD*. New York, NY: The Guilford Press, 2000.

PBS. "Federal Laws Pertaining to ADHD Diagnosed Children." Retrieved May 2006 (http://www.pbs.org/wgbh/pages/frontline/shows/medicating/schools/feds.html).

Reif, Sandra. *The ADD/ADHD Checklist*. San Francisco, CA: Jossey-Bass, 1997.

Schwab Learning. "Successful People with Learning Disabilities and/or AD/HD." SchwabLearning.org. January 22, 2001. Retrieved September 2006 (http://www.schwablearning.org/articles.asp?r=258).

Segal, Robert, MA, Jaelline Jaffe, Ph.D., and Jeanne Segal, Ph.D. "Medications for Treating ADHD: Risks, Benefits and Regimens." Helpguide.com. February 9, 2006. Retrieved September 2006 (http://www.helpguide.org/mental/adhd_medications.htm).

Strock, Margaret. "Attention Deficit Hyperactivity Disorder." National Institutes of Mental Health. February 17, 2006. Retrieved September 2006 (http://www.nimh.nih.gov/publicat/adhd.cfm#ref14).

Index

Photo Credits

Cover © www.istockphoto.com/Roberta Osborne; p. 5 © www. istockphoto. com/Lisse Gagne; p. 7 Anita Patterson Peppers/ Shutterstock.com; pp. 11, 12 PhotoCreate/Shutterstock.com; p. 15 © Chuck Burton/AP/Wide World Photos; p. 21 © www.istockphoto.com/ Daniel Lemay; p. 22 © Brendan Smialowski/Getty Images; p. 23 © www.istockphoto.com/Monika Adamczyk; p. 25 © Cordelia Molloy/ Photo Researchers, Inc.; p. 26 © www.istockphoto.com/David Lewis; p. 29 © Mississippi Press/William Colgin/AP/Wide World Photos; p. 33 © www.istockphoto.com/Graça Victoria; p. 36 Stephen Coburn/ Shutterstock.com; p. 39 Laurence Gough/Shutterstock.com; p. 44 © www.istockphoto.com/Jim Lopes; p. 49 © www.istockphoto.com/ ericsphotography; p. 50 Galina Barskaya/Shutterstock.com; p. 52 Jeff R. Clow/Shutterstock.com; p. 55 Keith Muratori/Shutterstock.com.

Designer: Evelyn Horovicz